Sharing the
NARNIA
EXPERIENCE

Sharing the
NARNIA
EXPERIENCE

A FAMILY GUIDE TO
C.S. LEWIS'S
The Lion, the Witch, and the Wardrobe

PAUL FRISKNEY

Project editor: Bruce Stoker
Cover design: Brand Navigation
Cover illustrator: Steve Gardner, PixelWorks Studio

ISBN 0-7847-1773-7

12	11	10	09	08	07	06	05	
9	8	7	6	5	4	3	2	1

※

DEDICATION

To Ann, Hannah, and Ben, with whom
I love sharing adventures.

※

ACKNOWLEDGEMENTS

A book such as this is not derived from the typical sources of
research and creativity. Instead, it comes from analysis and
application of the text. Therefore, I have to say that my first
level of gratitude has to be to C. S. Lewis himself, whose work
has captured my imagination and led to many enjoyable and
challenging reflections and discussions.

In a similar vein, I'm thankful to my mother, who taught
me to love reading, and my father, who taught me to analyze
and apply what I read. Thank you also to Ron Henderson,
whose course on Lewis's writing helped me to look at his work
with a larger perspective.

On a more immediate level, I offer my gratitude to Bruce
Stoker, who provided the impetus for this book after our
discussion about my reading the Narnia books with my son,
Ben, while we were living in Kosova. Thanks, as well, to others
at Standard Publishing who made it happen.

Finally, thank you to many family members, students, and
peers through the last twenty-five years or more with whom I
have enjoyed reading and discussing Lewis in many situations
both inside and outside of the classroom.

1

❆
CONTENTS

JUST SUPPOSE

"You have a good imagination!" That's a way to compliment a child or a way to criticize an adult. Fables and fairy tales that engage the imagination are meant only for children, right? C. S. Lewis disagreed. He wrote that he enjoyed fairy tales more as an adult because his life experience allowed him to put more into his reading of them than he was able to as a child.

Lewis's own imagination created a magical world in *The Chronicles of Narnia,* of which *The Lion, the Witch, and the Wardrobe* was the first book. And imagination allows people of all ages to connect to that world as we bring different aspects of our lives and understanding to the simple yet profound story.

Narnia originated, as most good fables do, from a combination of reality and imagination. During World War II, when many children were sent out of London into the countryside of England to protect them from nightly bombings, Lewis took several children into his home. He was delighted with them, and they seemed to be very eager to explore their new surroundings. That experience placed an image in Lewis's mind that began to grow and take shape.

The idea that Narnia began as a way to say something to children about Christianity is, according to Lewis, "moonshine." He began with an image of the fantasy world, and the Christian themes entered that world naturally since they were so significant in his thought system. The story that resulted is a marvelous joining of imagination and truth.

Lewis carefully pointed out that this joining is a "supposition" rather than an allegory. He didn't want his story to be read and broken apart to find out hidden connections. Instead, he constructed the world of Narnia out of his imagination and then "supposed" what God would do to redeem such a world if it existed. His hope was that the story would show an example of what God might do in such a circumstance.

> *Allegory*—
>
> A story in which all the elements (characters, places, activities) represent things outside of the story.

Perhaps it is this approach that allows the story to operate on so many different levels. Since it is a uniquely created world, it operates as a captivating story. But since it also draws on the truth of who God is and how he works, it offers a profound message to be considered by those who are open to it.

Many discussions of the story and of the themes present in it have been done in the more than fifty years since it first appeared in print. This book does not intend to go back over those studies. Instead, the goal is to approach the story as one of a group of readers, to ask questions and bring up ideas that spring from a direct reading of the story and from entering fully into the images and the supposition that guided Lewis's writing.

In the process, it is hoped that this book will act as a guide for a family or other group reading together through *The Lion, the Witch, and the Wardrobe*. With that in mind, this book will attempt to focus attention on the variety of ways that readers of different ages can experience Narnia for the first or the twentieth time.

The chapters of this book follow different segments of the adventure as it develops. Each chapter features a summary of the action in that portion of the book followed by these four sections:

Did You Know? Background information on important themes.

In the Family. The interactions of the brothers and sisters in the story and thoughts about what families can learn from them.

The People We Meet. Here the focus is on different characters in the story and the roles they play.

What If It Were You? Questions that your family can use as you discuss the book together.

The final chapter covers the same areas but deals with the book as a whole or can be used to discuss one of the film versions of the story.

So let's enter into the world of Narnia—a world of exciting adventures, engaging characters, striking symbols, and profound ideas! A world that connects to our imaginations, no matter their age or frequency of use. A world that we enter as we just suppose. . . .

One

DISCOVERIES

Chapters one & two

The Adventure So Far

Two brothers (Peter and Edmund) and their two sisters (Susan and Lucy) have been sent to stay in the country home of a professor. The professor is a kind man, but he doesn't interact much with the children on a daily basis, leaving them free to explore his huge home.

In their exploration, they discover a room that is empty except for a large wardrobe. The others leave the room disappointed, but Lucy stays to see what's inside the wardrobe. She is excited to find it full of fur coats, but the biggest surprise comes when she finds that the wardrobe has no back but leads into a snow-covered woods.

She soon meets Mr. Tumnus, who is a faun, half man and half goat. He is very careful to find out if Lucy is human and then invites her to his home and serves her tea. During tea, Lucy learns that the place where they are is called Narnia. Mr. Tumnus also tells her a little bit about what life is like there.

After they visit for a while, Mr. Tumnus starts crying and admits to Lucy that he has been ordered by the White Witch, the evil ruler of Narnia, to capture any humans who come and bring them to her. Since he has come to like Lucy, he can't go through with it, and he helps her go back to her own country.

> *Seeing Narnia—*
> The lamppost stands as a marker between Lucy's home world and the world of Narnia.

Did You Know?

During World War II, the time period when C. S. Lewis wrote *The Lion, the Witch, and the Wardrobe*, the city of London was bombed almost nightly by the Germans. Many children were sent from their homes in London to homes in the country in order to protect them. Some stayed with aunts and uncles or other relatives and friends, but often the people with whom they stayed were complete strangers who just wanted to help.

Of course, some situations were better than others, which is why Peter is so pleased with the situation they have with the Professor. C. S. Lewis himself had some children come to stay in his country home during the war.

Many homes in the past were built without closets, so people had to have somewhere else to store clothes, especially a place to hang their winter clothes during summertime. That's why many people had wardrobes. Wardrobes were kind of like wooden closets that weren't attached to the walls. Although they could be moved, they were usually pretty big and very heavy. The door was also usually heavy and had a fairly tight seal to keep out moths and other things that might damage the clothes. That's why Lewis keeps reminding his readers not to close the door of a wardrobe while they're inside.

Did you read the dedication in the front of *The Lion, the Witch, and the Wardrobe*? If so, you noticed that Lewis dedicated the book to Lucy Barfield, his goddaughter. That relationship may help to explain why the character who first enters Narnia and is the heroine of at least the first part of the story is named Lucy.

Children identify with Lucy as they read the book because she is the one who takes the first step into the great adventure. Lewis had no children of his own, but he seems to have had a soft spot in his heart for children in general.

In the Family

"Once there were four children." That's a very simple way to begin a book, but it brings us right into the heart of the family from the very beginning. We are introduced right away to the four children who will play important roles in the adventure, and we begin to get a sense of who they are and how they work together as a family.

We only learn a little about three of them in the first two chapters. Peter is basically the leader. He analyzes the situation and tells the others how they should see it. Susan tries to be a mother to the younger two. Edmund somewhat resents the fact that Peter and Susan are older, and he shows some signs of bad attitudes when things don't go exactly the way he wants them to go.

Much more focus is given to Lucy. Although she is the youngest of the four and at first is a bit scared of the new situation, she soon takes on the role of an adventurer. Her curiosity outweighs any shyness and leads her to keep going forward into Narnia, where she handles the unusual situations very well. When she meets Mr. Tumnus, we see clearly how her friendly nature and kindness win him over.

The People We Meet

The Professor is very old and has lots of shaggy white hair. The children like him almost immediately because he is so nice, but he's also funny-looking, which makes Lucy a little afraid of him and makes Edmund want to laugh. Some wonder if Lewis might be making fun of himself a little bit by the qualities he gives this character. Lewis also was an (at the time) unmarried professor living in a home out in the country.

As the first person we meet in Narnia, Mr. Tumnus introduces us to the odd combinations of ordinary and extraordinary things we will find there. In one sense, he is just like someone Lucy might have met on the street at home. He's holding an umbrella, and he has a scarf around his neck. He's carrying several packages as if he's been Christmas shopping.

But he's not the ordinary person on the street. He is a faun, human from the waist up and goat from the waist down. Fauns are found in Roman mythology and are similar to satyrs, which are found in Greek mythology. In both settings, they are usually characters who aren't very reliable, so it isn't too surprising when Mr. Tumnus turns out to be deceiving Lucy.

Item of Importance— The handkerchief of Lucy's that Mr. Tumnus keeps shows his connection to her. Watch for it to reenter the story.

However, we find out very quickly that he is really good at heart. Even before his reveals the truth to Lucy, the description of his cozy home lets us know that he's not really bad. After he admits that he's employed by the witch, he risks his own life to save Lucy.

What If It Were You?

❋ What do you think it would be like to be sent to live somewhere else and be separated from your family?

❋ How are the relationships within their family like and unlike the relationships in our family?

❈ When Lucy found that the wardrobe had no back, she felt "a little frightened" but also "inquisitive and excited." How do you think you would have felt? What do you think you would have done?

❈ What were the first things that Lucy noticed about Narnia? Do you think those things will turn out to be important?

❈ Why do you think Lucy doesn't seem to be afraid to talk to Mr. Tumnus?

❈ What do you notice in the description of Mr. Tumnus's home? What do those things tell you about him?

❈ What would you have said to Mr. Tumnus if you found out he was planning to capture you?

❈ Mr. Tumnus tells Lucy many things about what Narnia is like. Do you think she should believe him after he lied to her before?

❈ If you were Lucy, what would be the first thing you would tell your brothers and sister about Narnia?

❈ FOR OLDER FAMILY MEMBERS: If you were going to create a world in which to tell a story of evil, betrayal, goodness, and redemption, what kind of world would you create? What would the places and characters be like?

Two

EDMUND'S ENTRANCE

Chapters 3 & 4

Lucy returns from Narnia excited to share her adventure, but the others don't believe her because almost no time has passed since they saw her in the room with the wardrobe. Still, her excitement leads them to go check the wardrobe, but they find nothing but coats inside.

For a few days, Lucy is unhappy because no one believes her and Edmund is teasing her. Then, during a game of hide-and-seek, Lucy enters the wardrobe again. This time, Edmund goes in too, and he finds out that there really is a magical world inside the wardrobe.

But Edmund can't find Lucy once he's there. Instead, while he's wandering around, he meets a woman who calls herself a queen. At first, she is mean to Edmund, and he thinks that she might kill him. Then she changes all of a sudden and gives him something warm to drink and some dessert to eat. She asks him many questions and is especially interested in the fact that he has one brother and two sisters.

Edmund doesn't realize that the candy has a magic spell on it, so when he eats it, he can't think about anything else but wanting more of it. The woman says that he can't have any more until he comes to visit her at her house and brings his brother and sisters. She promises to make him a prince when he comes.

After the woman leaves, Lucy finds Edmund and tells him that she has been visiting Mr. Tumnus. She also tells him about the White Witch who pretends to be Queen of Narnia. Then they return home.

Lucy is very excited because now Edmund can tell the others about Narnia. But Edmund is feeling sick, and he isn't sure what to do since he knows that he's really on the Queen's side.

Seeing Narnia—

To help Edmund find her castle when he returns, the Queen tells him to look for the two hills that are on the other side of the woods from the lamppost. Can you picture standing at the lamppost and looking across Narnia to where the two hills are?

Did You Know?

Sledge is another word for *sleigh*. If you heard sleigh bells and saw a sleigh coming toward you being pulled by reindeer, who would you think it was? Santa Claus, right? Maybe that's why Edmund wasn't scared as he saw the sleigh coming toward him. But this sleigh had a dwarf instead of elves and a mean-looking lady instead of Santa. Edmund should have known better than to get into that sleigh!

Turkish Delight is a real dessert that's eaten in many countries. It's a sort of jellied candy that's cut up into cubes. Then it's usually covered with powdered sugar and sometimes nuts. It's very sweet! It's easy to understand why Edmund would get sick from eating pounds of it. The enchanted Turkish Delight in the story seems to work a lot like sin. Once Edmund has had some of it, he just wants more. He can't think about anything else. In fact, it makes him forget about the right things that he has been taught.

In the Family

When Lucy returns, the family situation becomes much more complicated. She tries to make Peter, Susan, and Edmund believe about Narnia, but they can't or won't. They make Lucy's life much harder for a while, but she sticks to the truth.

She shows us a good example of what we should do when we know something is true but others don't believe us. Even if people may make fun of us or don't want to be around us, following what's true is more important.

We learn a lot more about Edmund in these chapters. And what we learn doesn't make him look very good. We're told that he can be mean and that he makes fun of Lucy about Narnia before he goes there. When he follows Lucy through the wardrobe and can't find her, he thinks bad things about her and about all girls.

> "She could have made it up with the others quite easily at any moment if she could have brought herself to say that the whole thing was only a story made up for fun."

In Narnia, he gets into a sleigh with a stranger, and he eats much more candy than he knows that he should. He wants all the good things from the queen only for himself. He doesn't want Peter, Susan, and Lucy to get anything. And he doesn't want to admit that he was wrong even when he knows it's true.

The People We Meet

We know the White Witch is going to be important in the story because she's in the title of the book. Here, we see two sides of her. There's the queen who offers Edmund lots of wonderful things and makes him all kinds of promises. She's described as tall and beautiful, and she's dressed in white fur with a gold wand and a gold crown. She's riding in a fine-looking sleigh pulled by white reindeer with golden horns.

Then there's the witch that Lucy says Mr. Tumnus told her about. She's evil and bullies everyone else in Narnia. She has cast a spell on the whole land to make it "always winter but never

Christmas." Everyone is afraid of what she will do to people who don't do what she says.

They seem like two different people until we think about the way the beautiful woman claiming to be a queen treats Edmund before she finds out who he is. Then we know that even in Narnia, things aren't always what they seem to be. No matter how much she looks like a queen, she really is an evil witch. And that makes us wonder why she wants Edmund to bring his brother and sisters to her.

Along with the White Witch, we meet the dwarf driving her sleigh. He is short instead of tall like the witch, but he's also dressed in fur. He follows the witch's commands, but he doesn't seem to like it very much. And when he smiles at Edmund, Edmund doesn't like the smile. He definitely doesn't seem like someone you would want to trust!

What If It Were You?

❋ Have you ever told someone something that was true, but the person didn't believe you? How did you feel?

❋ How do you think Lucy felt when no one believed her?

❋ Do you think that she should have said that Narnia wasn't real so that her brothers and sister would have liked her again?

❋ Why do you think that Edmund was so mean to Lucy about Narnia?

❋ Is it hard for you to say that someone else was right and you were wrong? Why?

❋ Would you have gotten into the sleigh with the White Witch? What would you have done?

❋ What kinds of things do you like as much as Edmund liked Turkish Delight? What are you willing to do for those things? What aren't you willing to do?

❋ Do you ever say mean things to or about other people in the family? Do you tell them you're sorry if you do?

❋ Why do you think that the witch wants to know so much about Edmund's family? Is it all right for him to answer all of her questions?

❋ FOR OLDER FAMILY MEMBERS: How do you see the Turkish Delight being like sin and temptation? How are the effects on Edmund like the effects of sin? What can be done to resist that kind of temptation? What can we do to change direction and get back on track when we do sin?

Three

NEW PERSPECTIVE

Chapters 5 & 6

When Lucy and Edmund return from Narnia and catch up to Peter & Susan (who are still playing hide-and-seek), Lucy is excited to have Edmund back up what she said about Narnia. But Edmund decides to play a terrible trick on Lucy and to say that they had only been pretending.

His plan backfires a bit because he thinks that what he says will make the others think that he is much more grown up than Lucy. Instead, they are mad at him because they think that he has just been getting Lucy to pretend more. However, he does succeed in making Peter and Susan think that something is really wrong with Lucy.

For help, they turn to the Professor. Much to their surprise, he defends Lucy, pointing out that the only evidence against her story comes from Edmund, whom they realize has always been more likely to be lying than Lucy. The Professor tells them that until they have proof that she is not telling the truth, they should believe her. Meanwhile, he suggests that they all mind their own business.

That idea helps to keep things running more smoothly. No one talks about Narnia, so there aren't any fights about it. Then one day, as the children are trying desperately to keep out of the sight of the housekeeper and some visitors, they all enter the wardrobe and end up in Narnia.

When Peter and Susan realize that Lucy was telling the truth all along, they quickly apologize to her. Then Peter becomes very angry with Edmund when it becomes clear that he really was in Narnia with Lucy before. But instead of apologizing and trying to make things right, Edmund just starts planning how he can get back at the others.

Lucy is appointed the leader and takes them to Mr. Tumnus's house, but it has been torn apart. Within the torn furniture and pictures, they find a note saying that Mr. Tumnus has been taken captive as a traitor to the Queen. After a little discussion, Lucy, Susan, and Peter decide that they have to try to help Mr. Tumnus because he saved Lucy.

They don't really know where to go, but they follow a robin, who seems to be leading them through the woods. Then Edmund points out that they don't really know where they're going or if

Seeing Narnia—

Red things seem to stand out in Narnia among all of the white things. Earlier, we saw Mr. Tumnus's red scarf and the witch's red lips; now, it's the robin's red belly.

they can trust the robin. He also points out that they have no idea how to get home from where they are.

Did You Know?

In Great Britain, many castles and other buildings are hundreds of years old. Since they have connection to different events in history, people like to take tours of them. What makes it a little unusual is that often people still live there. How would you like to have someone touring your home while you're living there? That's how it is in the Professor's house. The Professor and Mrs. Macready are used to the practice, but it's something new to the children.

The discussion about Lucy that the Professor has with Peter and Susan includes an idea that C. S. Lewis also used in a more important discussion. The Professor says that Lucy is either lying or crazy or telling the truth. In talking about who Jesus is, Lewis would say that there are only three options for who he is: a liar, a lunatic, or Lord. Just as the Professor did with Lucy, Lewis ruled out the first two possibilities to show that the third is true.

In the first chapters of *The Lion, the Witch, and the Wardrobe*, Lewis has frequently used what's called foreshadowing, introducing things that will become more important later. Have you noticed how many times things related to Christmas have been mentioned? Have you started to wonder what this place called Cair Paravel is? What about this person named Fenris Ulf, who is the Captain of the Secret Police? What kind of creature do you think he is? Does the fact that the Old English spelling of *wolf* was *wulf* give you an idea?

> "Either your sister is telling lies, or she is mad, or she is telling the truth."

In the Family

Well, the children's time in the country certainly is not turning out to be as calm as they thought it was going to be at first. Peter and Susan are finding that things they assumed to be true aren't necessarily so. Lucy has been called a liar by the people that she's closest to. Edmund has been infected by enchanted Turkish Delight and is becoming more and more separated from his brother and sisters.

In these struggles, there are several things that we can learn from the family relationships. First, we see the value of the Professor's advice for the siblings to simply leave the topic of Narnia alone until the truth could come out on its own. Often, if we keep focusing on a point of disagreement, the problem just gets worse. Sometimes, the best thing to do, once everyone has had a chance to give an opinion, is to let things work themselves out.

On the negative side, we see in Edmund what happens to someone who doesn't care whether he hurts others and just tries to make himself look more important. He not only causes pain to the others, especially Lucy, but he makes things miserable for himself, too. And then when the truth comes out (which it nearly always does), it just causes him more problems and increases the conflict with his brother and sisters.

The People We Meet

OK, a house isn't really a person, but in this part of the story, the Professor's house really seems to become a character of its own. The Professor tells Peter and Susan that the house has secrets that even he doesn't know about. Then, when the children are trying to escape from Mrs. Macready and the tourists, the magic of the house makes it seem as if the children are surrounded. The house practically forces them into the wardrobe so that they enter the world of Narnia together.

Mrs. Macready herself takes on more of a role as well. The children met her when they arrived at the Professor's house, but they try to stay out of her way, especially when she's giving tours of the house. Unlike the professor, Mrs. Macready doesn't like children. That dislike along with Mrs. Macready's stern face helps to explain why the children are so intent on getting away from her that they are willing to go into the place that they have all been avoiding even talking about.

What If It Were You?

❈ Why do you think that Edmund decides to lie about his first trip to Narnia?

❊ Have you ever wanted to lie about something to make yourself look better to other people? What happened?

❊ Why were Peter and Susan so surprised by what the Professor said about believing Lucy? Do you think that what he said makes sense?

❊ Are there times that our family would have been better off not talking about something so that we didn't make each other angry?

❊ How does each of the children act when they go into Narnia? Are you surprised by any of their responses?

❊ The children discuss whether it's all right to take the coats to keep them warm. Do you think that they should have taken the coats? Why or why not?

❊ When they realize they don't have any food, they consider going back to get some, but they are afraid they won't be able to get back into Narnia. Would you have gone back for food or not?

❊ Would you have followed the robin the way that the children did? Would you have felt differently if it were a different bird or animal?

❊ How would you have felt when you realized you weren't sure how to get home? Would you have started home then, or would you have kept following the robin?

✻ FOR OLDER FAMILY MEMBERS: Edmund brings up the question of how to know which side is the right side. How do you determine what's right? Do you think there are definite sides in our world as there seem to be in Narnia? What passages of Scripture can help you to know what's right? (Try 1 John 4 as a starting point.)

LEARNING ABOUT NARNIA

Chapters 7, 8 & 9

The Adventure Continues

The next person the children meet in Narnia is Mr. Beaver. At first they're not sure whether to trust him, but they finally decide that they don't really have any other choice. He leads them through the thick woods until they come out at the other side and reach a big river, which has a dam that Mr. Beaver has built with a house in it.

In the house, the children meet Mrs. Beaver, and they help the Beavers as they go about fixing a wonderful meal that satisfies the appetites of the very hungry children. After dinner, the Beavers begin to reveal different facts about what's happening in Narnia. Most significantly, they begin to tell the children about

> ### *Seeing Narnia—*
> The snow falling everywhere helps to keep visitors away from the Beavers' home and to cover the tracks that the children have made so that no one can follow them.

Aslan, the Lion King of Narnia, who has just entered the land.

When Edmund has finished eating and has heard all that he thinks he needs to hear, he decides to leave the others so that he can find the Witch.

The others are so focused on what the Beavers are saying that they don't notice the fact that he leaves. Unfortunately, when he gets outside, he realizes that he has forgotten his coat and that it's beginning to get dark. But there's no way he can go back at that point.

After a short time, the others discover that Edmund is missing. Peter, Susan, and Lucy run outside to try to find him, but when they come back in, Mr. Beaver makes them realize that Edmund is not lost but has gone to betray them to the Witch. The Beavers tell the children that their only hope is to meet up with Aslan before the Witch can cut them off from him.

Meanwhile, Edmund is undergoing a long, cold, wet journey to get to the Witch's house. He does a lot of thinking, trying to convince himself that he's doing the right thing. When he arrives, he's not sure, at first, whether he wants to be there after all. He is frightened for a long time by a lion that he sees in the entrance to the courtyard until he realizes that it is a statue.

As he goes on in, he sees all kinds of creatures that the Witch has turned into stone. Just as he is starting to get used to the statues, one of the animals, a huge wolf, turns out to be alive, scaring Edmund again.

When Edmund is finally taken inside the palace, it isn't any happier looking. It's still dark, and there are more statues, including one that Edmund thinks might be Mr. Tumnus.

The Witch is very angry that Edmund has come alone, but she is very interested in the fact that his brother and sisters are in Narnia. She reacts even more when she hears that Aslan has returned.

> *Hearing Narnia—*
> The first time Edmund met the Witch, he knew she was coming by the sound of sleigh bells. The harness without bells means the she's hoping to sneak up on someone!

Did You Know?

As promised, the handkerchief that Lucy gave to Mr. Tumnus shows up again in the possession of Mr. Beaver. He calls it his "token." That's a different use of the word *token* than we're used to. In the past, a token was an object that was used to guarantee a person's identity or authority or relationship to someone else. The fact that Mr. Beaver has the handkerchief and knows that it belonged to Lucy shows that Mr. Tumnus trusted him with that information. That lets the children know that they can trust him, too.

The Beavers begin to introduce the children to rhymes and sayings that have been known in Narnia for many, many years. These sayings tell about signs of things that will happen in Narnia in the future. To us, some of the "rhymes" may not seem to rhyme for two main reasons.

First, some things are pronounced differently in England than they are in America, even though both countries speak English. For example, people in England say the word *again* in a way that makes it rhyme with *mane*. Also, one kind of rhyme is based on how words look rather than how they sound. It's called "eye rhyme," and according to it, *done* can be said to rhyme with *bone* and *throne*.

But more important than the rhyming words are the things that the rhymes and sayings tell about what will happen. From them, we learn that Aslan's presence will help to make things right in Narnia. He will end sorrow and bring back spring. We also learn about the importance of the children's coming to Narnia. If the four of them sit on the four thrones in the castle of Cair Paravel, it will mean the end of the Witch's power and even of the Witch herself.

We find out some interesting information about the Witch from the Beavers. The children have been assuming that she is human, but she's not. She is described as being a Jinn and being a descendent of Adam's first wife, Lilith.

Lewis draws from different legends in this description of the Witch. Lilith is a character found in Jewish rabbinical legend. In that legend, she is presented as the first wife of Adam. She is then replaced by Eve and becomes an evil spirit. The Jinn, on the other hand, can be found in Muslim demonology as evil spirits that inhabit the earth, take various forms, and have magical powers.

Obviously, all of these connections just emphasize the fact that the Witch is indeed evil. As Mr. Beaver points out, humans can be either good or bad, but things that pretend to be human but aren't are always bad news.

Edmund's dreams of being a king mean even more when we remember that both the character and the author who created him are British. In America, we think about kings sometimes, but they don't seem very real because they're not a part of the way things work here.

Edmund has a very specific idea in mind when he thinks about being a king. That's why he talks about fixing the roads in Narnia (as well as making life difficult for people he thinks haven't been nice to him). He doesn't have any more trouble picturing what a king can do than we have picturing what a president can do.

In the Family

This section starts with a positive image of family. As the children realize that they are lost and that they have to trust someone to help them, Peter reminds them all to stay close together because together they will be more able to take care of themselves. That togetherness takes them through their first meeting with Mr. Beaver, the long hike in the woods, and even preparations for dinner.

Unfortunately, that's as long as it lasts. Edmund, whose taste buds have been changed by his tasting of the enchanted Turkish Delight, can't really enjoy the meal. The separation increases when the children hear Aslan's name. Peter, Susan, and Lucy all have wonderfully positive responses to his name, but Edmund feels horror. From that point on, they hear things very differently.

> "There's nothing that spoils the taste of good ordinary food half so much as the memory of bad magic food."

As Edmund makes his way to the Witch's castle, he builds up his negative feelings toward the others. He blames Peter for the problems Edmond has along the way even though Peter doesn't know where Edmond's gone. Edmond doesn't believe that the Witch will turn his brother and sisters into stone, but he doesn't want her to be nice to them either.

The other children feel differently about Edmund. Although they don't like some of the things that he has said and done, they are very worried about him when they realize he's gone. They also don't want to believe that he would betray them to the Witch, but deep inside, they know that it's true.

The People We Meet

As the children learn more about Narnia, they find out just how different it is from their home. That includes the kinds of people they meet there. Not only are the animals much larger than they are in England, but they can talk, too. Even the trees are listening and take sides either with the animals or with the Witch.

Except for the way they look, Mr. and Mrs. Beaver sound like the ultimate wonderful grandparents. They have a cozy little cottage by the river. Mr. Beaver takes Peter fishing with him, and Mrs. Beaver lets the others help her as she fixes them a wonderful meal. They sit with the children in the living room telling stories and reciting poems.

But the Beavers are more than just nice people (as important as that is). They give the children very important information that they need to know. They also provide direction and protection for the children in a place where the children couldn't manage alone. They know how important the children are to the future of Narnia, and they want to do everything they can to help.

Of course, the most important character we are introduced to in this section (although we haven't actually met him yet) is Aslan. At first, the Beavers assume that the children must know who he is, but when they find out that that is not true, they let them know that he is the great Lion King of Narnia. He comes rarely to Narnia, but he is said to be there now.

The Beavers are offended when the children ask if Aslan is a man because he has much more power than any man could have. He has the power to save and to set things right. In response to Lucy's question, they say that he's not safe, but he's good. In other words, he has great power, so he shouldn't be taken for

> "It is he, not you, that will save Mr. Tumnus."

granted, but he uses that power for good. In fact, his power is so great that nobody can stand up to him, including the Witch.

Two names that we heard earlier come to mean more in this section. We find out that Cair Paravel is a castle by the sea that is important to Narnia becoming what it is meant to be. On the other hand, we find out that Fenris Ulf is indeed a horrible wolf that serves the Witch.

What If It Were You?

❋ How would you have decided whether or not to trust Mr. Beaver?

❋ What details do you remember about the Beavers' house? Does it remind you of any place that you've been before?

❋ Peter said that if they stuck together, they would be better able to take care of themselves. Can you think of some times when it is especially important that we work together as a family?

❋ The Beavers talk about old sayings that predict what will happen when Aslan comes to Narnia. Can you think of Scriptures written before Jesus was born that tell about his coming? (See Isaiah 7:14 and Micah 5:2 for starters.)

❋ Each of the children had a different reaction to hearing Aslan's name. Why do you think that's true? What do you think Aslan will be like when he comes into the story?

❋ Why can't Edmund enjoy the dinner at the Beavers' house? Have you ever had a time when something you had done wrong made it difficult for you to enjoy something that you normally would have enjoyed?

❋ What is Edmund thinking about as he heads toward the Witch's house? Why does he blame everything on Peter?

❋ How would you have felt if you had gotten to the Witch's house and saw what Edmund saw? Would you have wanted to go in or wanted to leave?

❋ How do you think that Peter, Susan, and Lucy felt when they realized that Edmund was going to tell the Witch about them? Have you ever had a time when someone you loved did something that hurt you? How did you feel?

> "Fortunate favourite of the Queen—or else not so fortunate."

❋ For older family members: Fenris Ulf points out that there is a question of whether Edmund is in a good position in his relationship with the queen. What do you think Fenris Ulf means by that? Why do we sometimes try to convince ourselves that something is good for us when we know it isn't? What areas of your life are the hardest for you to be honest about?

Five

ON THE MOVE

Chapters 10 & 11

As our title for this section indicates, many of the characters are on the move in this part of the adventure. The Beavers take Peter, Susan, and Lucy toward the place where they will meet Aslan. The Witch heads out in her sleigh with the dwarf and Edmund to try to intercept them. She also sends Fenris Ulf and another wolf to the Beavers' house to try to catch them before they leave. Most significantly, Aslan is on the move. Even though we don't see him in this section, we see evidence of his presence.

The exit from the Beavers' home is slowed down a little by Mrs. Beaver. Mr. Beaver and the three children become frustrated and try to get her just to leave, but she very logically sticks to her plan to put together things they will need on the trip. Each person is given a bag to carry on the journey so that they won't be without food and other supplies.

On the other hand, much to Edmund's dismay, the Witch doesn't seem to be interested in food at all. Instead of the Turkish Delight he is expecting, all she offers him is water and bread so stale that he can hardly eat it. They set out on their trip with no food or supplies. The Witch is only interested in catching the others as quickly as possible.

Mr. Beaver leads his group across paths that the Witch's sleigh can't possibly travel so that they don't have to worry about running into her. When night comes, he shows them an old beaver hiding place where they can sleep. Even though they sleep very well, it seems too short when they wake up the next morning.

As soon as they're awake, they hear sleigh bells, and they are all afraid that it is the Witch coming to get them. (Of course, we know it's not the Witch because the Witch is using the harness without bells.) The rest of the group waits in the cave while Mr. Beaver goes to check out the situation. They think he has been captured when they hear voices, but then, they hear Mr. Beaver telling them to come out of the cave because everything is fine.

The visitor turns out to be Father Christmas (Santa Claus). He is the first big sign that the Witch's power is breaking since she declared that it would be always winter and *never* Christmas. The children receive gifts from Father Christmas that he tells them must be used in special ways. Then, he is gone almost before the others realize he's leaving.

Edmund's experience with the Witch is quite different from what the others are doing. Since he's riding in a sleigh while it's snowing and he doesn't have a coat, he's very cold and wet. He's also hungry, and the Witch is getting meaner and meaner. Edmund is beginning to see that he has definitely made the wrong choice.

Any doubts he had about his choice are gone after they come to the site of a Christmas party. There's a squirrel family along with two satyrs, a dwarf, and a fox. The Witch is so angry on hearing that they have been given gifts by Father Christmas that she turns them and all their food into stone.

There trip gets worse and worse as the weather gets warmer and warmer. Eventually, the sleigh can't go any farther, so all three have to walk. Edmund has his hands tied behind his back, so it is hard to keep his balance on the slippery ground, and the dwarf sometimes hits him with his whip. Meanwhile, all around them, more signs of spring are showing themselves.

Did You Know?

Father Christmas is what Santa Claus is called in Great Britain. Since, as Lewis points out, it's only in Narnia that a character like Santa Claus can be seen, it's not surprising that he's pictured a little differently in some countries. The usual British picture of Father Christmas is that he wears a long, bright red robe with a fur-lined hood rather than a hat.

However, many parts of the description of Father Christmas match the one we normally think of with Santa Claus. He still rides in a sleigh pulled by reindeer. He has a magic bag that contains presents for him to give away. Also, he's not stopped by locked doors when he wants to leave a present in a home.

Many countries have different traditions about Santa Claus. They call him by different names, have different ideas of when and how he comes, and expect different kinds of presents from him. A fun family project would be to find out some of these different stories.

Father Christmas is not the only sign of the change that's coming over Narnia because Aslan is near. In fact, even before the change begins to take place, the Witch knows that it's coming. That's why she has to take her sleigh a long way to the west to cross the river. If she had been sure that she could keep it frozen, she would have been able to cross it anywhere.

As the sleigh is traveling, Edmund feels the snow getting wetter and the air getting warmer. It gets foggier and foggier, and he can hear running water. Then, the sunlight comes, and he starts seeing patches of green grass. Eventually, there are flowers and birds singing. As the dwarf points out, "This is no thaw. This is *spring*."

Lewis gives us different reminders, sometimes in a humorous way, of the fact that he is telling the story of a completely different world. When Mr. Beaver uses the wrong form of a pronoun in a sentence, the narrator tells us that he is simply being true to the way beavers talk—in Narnia, that is, since they don't usually talk in our world. He makes the same kind of distinction when he points out that only in the world of Narnia can Santa Claus be seen.

While this is just a fun part of the story for the younger family members, it reminds those who are older of something that's very important for Lewis. This world is a completely different one. He doesn't want us to try to draw a lot of parallels between characters in the story and characters in our own world. As we discussed in the introduction, this is not an allegory but a supposition.

He wants us to join him in supposing this world much different from our own. Then, he wants us to watch with him to see what God will do to save this world just as we already know what he has done to save ours.

In the Family

This section shows a huge difference between what Peter, Susan, and Lucy are experiencing and what Edmund is going through. The first three have a hard trip carrying heavy packs, but they have many positives in their experience. They are being protected, led, and fed by the Beavers. They sleep fairly comfortably snuggled among the warm furs in the cave.

Most significantly, they meet Father Christmas, which would be a tremendous thing for any child. The experience makes them feel both glad and serious. Those feelings are made stronger by the gifts he gives them, which are obviously very important and which we can expect to see later in the story.

Peter is given a shield that has a red lion on it. Long ago, when shields were used in battles, the picture on the shield showed

> "They are tools not toys."

which side the fighter was on. Peter is on the Lion's side. He's also given a sword to use in battle.

Susan and Lucy are told that they won't fight in the battle, so the weapons they're given (bow and arrows for Susan and a dagger for Lucy) are only to be used for defense in extreme situations. In addition, Susan is given an ivory horn, and Lucy has a bottle, possibly made of diamond, that has powerful medicine inside it.

We'll have to wait to see how these gifts are used in the rest of the adventure.

Edmund's experience is much different. He has no one caring for him. The Witch is mean and doesn't offer him anything to keep him from being cold and hungry. At first, it seems as if at least his trip is going to be easier than the way the others are traveling, but then even that goes bad.

Edmund is learning an important lesson the hard way: when you think only about yourself, it can really backfire on you. In fact, a big turning point comes for Edmund when he sees what happens to the squirrel family and their friends. The narrator says, "Edmund for the first time in this story felt sorry for someone besides himself." That change in perspective starts other big changes happening. He feels excitement over the fact that winter is ending, even though he's not exactly sure why he feels that way.

The picture we see here of Edmund shows the way that God begins to work on our hearts to lead us to him. We have to break out of our self-centered world and begin to allow God to "thaw" our hearts so that we can recognize him for who he is and accept what he has to offer us.

The People We Meet

We've already said a great deal about Father Christmas, but obviously, he's a very important person in this section of the book. Peter, Susan, and Lucy don't respond exactly as we might expect them to when they meet him. Besides feeling glad, they feel "solemn" or serious. It isn't all happiness. They realize how important it is that he has finally come to Narnia, so they know that everything is moving toward the final confrontation between the forces of good and the forces of evil there. That leads them to stand quietly during the experience.

Besides the gifts for the children, Father Christmas also has gifts for the Beavers. For the practical Mrs. Beaver, there is the practical gift of a sewing machine. As might be expected, she responds practically by pointing out that the house is locked. Mr. Beaver receives help in the most significant aspect of his life's work: dam building. It leaves the normally talkative beaver speechless.

Of course, we already know a lot about the Witch, but we see her fully in this part of the story. She is hateful and cruel. She wants to destroy anything that threatens to take away her power. She can't stand for anyone to disagree with her. She'll pretend to be whatever people want her to be until she has them on her side, and then she uses them in whatever way works best for her.

Through her, we are given a tremendous warning to be careful whom we trust and what ideas we listen to. Edmund thinks that he will be a king, but he ends up with his hands tied behind his back, walking through the mud, being hit by a whip. The dwarf thinks he can give the Witch advice, but she quickly reminds him that he is just her slave. We think that we can do whatever we want and be able to control the situation, but it doesn't work out that way. We end up the losers.

> "Are you my councillor or my slave?"

The characters at the Christmas party are certainly a mixed group. There's a squirrel family and a fox, who might seem likely to be enemies themselves, but they are also joined by a dwarf and two satyrs. Obviously, the change that is coming over Narnia is one that will bring people together no matter how different they might seem to be.

What If It Were You?

❋ If you had been part of the group going to meet Aslan, do you think you would have been more like Mrs. Beaver (trying to get together everything you might need) or more like the others (wanting to leave as soon as possible)?

❋ What helps Lucy keep going even though the pack is so heavy and she is so tired? What helps you do things that you know you need to do even when they are hard?

❋ What is the reason we celebrate Christmas? Do you see ways that what happened on the first Christmas is like what happens in the story when Father Christmas comes?

❋ How would you have felt if you had heard the sleigh bells and thought the Witch was coming after you? What would you have done?

❋ If you could pick one of the gifts that Father Christmas gave, which one would it be? Why?

❋ What is Edmund finding out about the Witch? Why doesn't he run away from her?

❋ Why do you think that Fenris Ulf and the dwarf let the Witch boss them around?

❋ How would you have felt if you saw the Witch turn the squirrels and the others at the Christmas party into stone? Would you have tried to stop her the way that Edmund did?

❀ Have you ever realized that you made a mistake (as Edmund has)? What did you do to make it right?

❀ FOR OLDER FAMILY MEMBERS: How is the situation of Edmund and the Witch similar to what we experience with temptation and sin? What develops in the process of sin? What can happen to change our perspective? (Use Scriptures such as John 8:34-36 and James 1:14-16 to help.)

---------------- *Six* ----------------

FIGHT TO THE FINISH?

Chapters 12, 13 & 14

The Adventure Continues

The two groups are still headed by different routes to the Stone Table. The Beavers, Peter, Susan, and Lucy are excited to see all the changes that are taking place as the weather warms. Even though the trip is incredibly long, they don't mind it so much now that all of the beauty of nature is appearing around them. They also realize that they don't have to hurry as much now that the Witch's sleigh won't work without snow.

The travelers have had to change their course since the melting snow has flooded the river valley they were walking in. At the end of a long day of hiking, they climb up a hill that

Seeing Narnia—

As the Witch's spell breaks, the true beauty of Narnia shines through with sparkling sunshine, green meadows, huge beds of flowers, and beautiful wooded areas filled with many different kinds of birds.

is almost too much for them. But just as Lucy thinks she can't go any farther, they reach the top.

What they see at the top makes the trip worth all the trouble. First, they see the sea far off to the east. Then they notice, right in the middle of the open area on top of the hill, the Stone Table. Off to one side is a pavilion or big open tent. It glows in the setting sun and has a banner with a red lion (like the one on Peter's shield).

But most of all, Aslan is there, the great Lion King that they have been waiting to meet. However, at first, they are all afraid to talk to him. Each tries to get someone else to go first, but finally, Peter summons up the courage to speak to Aslan, who welcomes them all and asks where Edmund is.

Aslan then sends Susan and Lucy off with some women who will take care of them, and he leads Peter for a view of the faraway castle of Cair Paravel. To Peter, who sees it in the light of the setting sun, it looks like a "star resting on the seashore." But as they are looking, they hear Susan's horn sounding, and Aslan sends Peter to save the girls.

Susan is really the one who is in danger since she has been chased up a tree by Fenris Ulf. Peter can tell by looking at her that she is about to faint, and if she does, she will fall right to the place where the wolf is standing. Peter acts quickly and uses his sword to kill the enemy and save his sister. Then Aslan sends off a group of his followers to rescue Edmund.

Meanwhile, the Witch has decided that she must kill Edmund to make sure that not all four thrones at Cair Paravel will be filled by humans.

> "Peter did not feel very brave; indeed, he felt he was going to be sick. But that made no difference to what he had to do."

She is just getting ready to do it when the wolf who had been with Fenris Ulf comes to tell her that the captain has been killed. She sends that wolf off to gather the rest of her followers while she has Edmund tied to a tree and sharpens her knife.

Just as she is ready to kill him, the rescue party sent by Aslan arrives to save Edmund. They untie him and take him back to Aslan, but the Witch and the dwarf escape because she is able to make them appear to be a boulder and a tree stump.

The next morning, the brothers and sisters are reunited after Aslan has had a long talk with Edmund, who apologizes to the others. But they don't have much time to enjoy their reunion because the Witch shows up to claim her right to kill Edmund. It seems that the Deep Magic, which the Emperor-Beyond-the-Sea set up to govern Narnia, gives the Witch the right to a kill for every betrayal.

Of course, that causes great concern for Peter, Susan, and Lucy. But Edmund seems strangely unafraid as he just focuses his attention on Aslan. The Lion King has everyone move back so that he can talk to the Witch alone. Then he announces to the crowd that she has given up her claim to Edmund, and she leaves.

That night, Susan and Lucy can't sleep, and they follow Aslan as they see him leaving the camp. Soon they are walking with him and comforting the sad Lion until he tells them to stop and makes them promise not to come after him. From their spot in hiding, the girls watch as the Witch and her helpers tie up Aslan, cut off his mane, put a muzzle on him, and kill him.

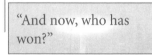
"And now, who has won?"

Just before he dies, the Witch tells him that he has done it for nothing. Once he is dead, she will simply kill all of the others, including Edmund, and rule Narnia forever.

Did You Know?

As the followers of Aslan and the followers of the Witch form into two separate armies, we get a fuller picture of all of the kinds of creatures that are involved in the imaginary world that Lewis has created.

Some are taken from mythology, such as Dryads (tree nymphs) and Naiads (water nymphs) and centaurs (half man/ half horse). Others come from legends and fairy tales. There are dwarfs, giants, and ogres. Also, different animals are involved, including wolves, eagles, and, of course, lions. Lewis goes on to say that the Witch's forces also included some creatures so horrible that, if they were described in the book, children wouldn't be allowed to read it. All in all, there is a great picture of the complete forces of good and evil lining up against each other for the final showdown.

The pavilion that the children see near the Stone Table is the kind of picture that is often given of what is set up for a king or another leader who is traveling on a mission. The tent provides a place of shelter for the king and his followers that can easily be moved from place to place as they travel on. The banners flying would invite their friends to join them and warn their enemies to stay away.

In the Family

Through the brothers and sisters, we learn some lessons about responsibility and forgiveness in this section. First, when Peter is telling Aslan about Edmund's betrayal, Peter recognizes his own fault in the situation. Clearly, Edmund made his own choices, but Peter is humble and honest enough to admit that he could have helped but, instead, made things worse by his attitude toward and treatment of Edmund.

When the children are reunited after Edmund's talk with Aslan, Edmund apologizes to them all, and they all forgive him. Aslan reminds them that there is no need to talk about it anymore.

> "'Here is your brother,' he said, 'and—there is no need to talk to him about what is past.'"

They are to resist the temptation we all have to bring such things back up whenever there are new problems. Forgiveness means letting go of those past hurts forever.

The People We Meet

A sure sign that we are reaching the most significant part of the book is the fact that Aslan finally comes on the scene. We have heard a lot about him, and now we finally see him. In fact, seeing him is nothing to take lightly. Peter, Susan, and Lucy had heard a lot about him, but they are a bit afraid in his presence. Even Mr. Beaver is afraid to speak to him. Later, the Witch isn't able to look Aslan in the eyes.

> "People who have never been in Narnia sometimes think that a thing cannot be good and terrible at the same time."

However, the fear doesn't last for those who are on Aslan's side. Once Peter and the girls hear Aslan speak, they are no longer afraid. After Edmund spends some time with Aslan, he keeps his eyes focused on the Lion and is unconcerned even when the Witch is threatening his life.

These different feelings about Aslan help us to begin to see what a complex and important figure he is in the story. That leads us to think back to Lewis' statement that he is supposing what God would do to redeem a world like Narnia if such a world existed. Aslan is obviously a part of that redemption.

Aslan is calm in the midst of the Witch's claim to authority, saying that "all names will soon be restored to their proper owners" and refusing to be concerned about "noises." He knows the Deep Magic better than anyone, and he willingly offers himself in Edmund's place. In spite of having all the power necessary to destroy the Witch and her followers, Aslan allows himself to be humiliated, tortured, and killed by them.

The parallels between Aslan and Jesus are many. That shouldn't surprise us since the only thing Lewis had on which to base his supposing was the way that God chose to redeem this world: through the willing sacrifice of Jesus. Aslan even dies in the same position that Jesus did: looking up to God.

What If It Were You?

❋ What changes do you notice around our house when winter changes to spring? What would you think if all the changes happened in one day?

❋ Why were the Beavers and the children afraid to speak to Aslan? Do you think you would have been afraid?

❋ Peter was the one who finally spoke up. Who do you think would have spoken first in our family?

❋ Can you think of a time when something you did or said was part of what someone else did wrong (the way Peter admitted that he was part of Edmund's problem)? Did you admit that you were wrong, too?

❊ Aslan, Peter, Susan, and Lucy all forgave Edmund. Do you forgive people when they are really sorry for what they've done, or do you keep holding it against them?

❊ How is Aslan like Jesus? (See Luke 23, 24 and Philippians 2:5-11 for some ideas.)

❊ What do you think it would be like to meet Jesus face to face? What would you say to him?

❊ Has there ever been anything that bothered you enough that you couldn't sleep? What did you do about it? Did you talk to anyone?

❊ How would you have felt if you had watched what happened to Aslan the way that Susan and Lucy did?

❊ FOR OLDER FAMILY MEMBERS: We haven't yet heard the full effect of what Aslan has done for Edmund. What are the results of Jesus' sacrifice for us? (See 2 Corinthians 5:14-19 and Hebrews 9:11-15 to get started.)

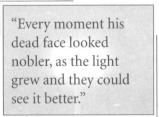

----- *Seven* -----

LIFE RETURNS

Chapters 15 & 16

As Susan and Lucy continue to watch from their hiding place, the Witch and her followers celebrate the death of Aslan and head off to kill the rest of his army. After the others leave, the girls go up the hill to the Stone Table. They take the muzzle off Aslan, stroke his fur, and cry.

They want to take off the ropes with which Aslan is tied as well, but the knots are too tight. Eventually, the job is taken care of by hundreds of field mice who come and chew through the ropes so that Aslan's body is freed.

> "Every moment his dead face looked nobler, as the light grew and they could see it better."

Morning is coming, and the girls realize that they are cold and stiff, so they go walking around. Their walk is brought to an end by a great cracking sound, and when they return, they find that the Stone Table has cracked all of the way through and Aslan's body is gone.

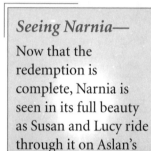

Seeing Narnia—

Now that the redemption is complete, Narnia is seen in its full beauty as Susan and Lucy ride through it on Aslan's back. By comparison, the Witch's castle looks like a toy.

Then they see Aslan himself, bigger than he had ever been. At first, the girls are afraid that he might be a ghost, but they soon realize that he is alive, and the three run around and play together. When they finish, the girls are no longer cold or tired or hungry. Aslan has them climb onto his back, and they race off to help the others against the Witch. Their first stop is the Witch's castle. One by one, all of the creatures that the Witch had turned into statues are changed back by Aslan's breath. They search the whole castle until they're sure that everyone, including Mr. Tumnus, has been saved.

Then they all head off toward the battle. When they arrive, Peter and those fighting with him seem to be having a very hard time. The Witch has turned several into statues. The ones remaining seem to be nearly worn out, and Peter is using his sword to fight against the Witch and her stone knife. Aslan has the girls get off of his back immediately, and he leaps on top of the Witch, who looks at him terrified and amazed. The appearance of Aslan and his reinforcements brings a cheer from

Peter and the others, which mixes with all of the other sounds of the battle to make a tremendous noise.

Did You Know?

In the picture of Aslan after he comes back to life, Lewis brings to completion a theme that he has been developing since we began hearing about Aslan. That theme has to do with how Aslan inspires both joy and fear. When Susan and Lucy see Aslan alive again for the first time, we're told that they are almost as afraid as they are happy. The mixture of feelings continues as they stay with him. When they're playing together, Lucy can't decide if it's "more like playing with a thunderstorm or playing with a kitten." And when their friend lets out a roar, they have to cover their ears and they don't dare to look at his face.

When the Stone Table breaks in half, it brings to mind something that happened when Jesus was crucified. At the moment of Jesus' death, the veil in the temple was torn from the top to the bottom (Matthew 27:51). That tearing represented the removal of the separation between God and man. Perhaps the breaking of the Stone Table is Lewis's way of showing that the same thing has happened for the creatures in Narnia. Another comparison could be the stone that was placed in front of Jesus' tomb. In the process of his resurrection, the stone was moved aside.

The fact that the mice are the ones who remove the ropes that tie Aslan reminds us of another story. In an old fable, a lion captures a mouse to eat it. The mouse begs the lion to spare his life and promises that he will help him in the future. The lion can't imagine how a tiny mouse could possibly help him, but he decides to let it go anyway. Later, when the lion has been captured by hunters, the mouse chews through the ropes of the net and frees the lion.

The point in that story is that even those who seem unimportant can do very important things. The same thing is true here. Susan and Lucy at first think that the mice mean to harm Aslan, but they soon realize that they really are helping in a way that the girls were unable to.

Lewis has a great way of providing comparisons to things we know to help us understand things that we couldn't possibly have experienced since they are only possible in Narnia. This section has two great examples.

First, to help us understand what it was like for Susan and Lucy to ride on Aslan's back, he compares it to riding on horseback. The ride is perhaps the greatest experience the girls have in Narnia because it has all of the positives of riding a horse without any of the negatives. It is the smoothest, fastest, most comfortable ride imaginable.

Another comparison is used to show what it is like when the statues change back to their living forms. Lewis compares it to lighting a fire. At first, there's no evidence that anything has happened. Then, a small flame begins to grow until it takes over the whole material that is burning. The statues follow that same kind of gradual development as they change from stone to living bodies.

The Witch is ultimately defeated because she knows only the Deep Magic, not the deeper magic. Her knowledge goes back only to when time began. Aslan's understanding goes back farther so that he knows all the truth. Since he has greater power and greater understanding, the Witch cannot possibly defeat him.

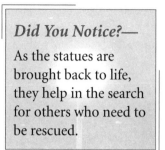

Did You Notice?—

As the statues are brought back to life, they help in the search for others who need to be rescued.

Similarly, in our own world, there are times when evil seems to be winning. But the forces of evil are completely limited to time. They cannot look back into eternity before time. Also, in the eternity of Heaven, elements of evil will have no place.

In the Family

For most of this section, the family is limited to Susan and Lucy since Peter and Edmund don't appear until the very end of chapter 16 when we get to the battle scene. Still, we can learn an important lesson about family from looking at the time that the two girls spend together here.

They share all kinds of emotions and experiences in a very short space of time. First, they are incredibly sad about Aslan's death, so sad that they don't even feel fear as they normally would when the Witch and her evil creatures run right past them. Then, the girls wander the hillside together feeling rather cold and numb after their loss.

After they see Aslan alive, they share the joy of that time and the fun of running and playing together with the Lion. Then they ride together on Aslan's back, with Lucy holding on to Susan, for the greatest adventure of their lives. Sharing all of those experiences must bring the girls closer together than they have ever been before.

In our families, we will also go through many different experiences. Sometimes, they will seem overwhelmingly sad, and other times, they will be joyful. But in all of them, we benefit from sharing them together rather than having to go through them alone.

The People We Meet

We continue to see new creatures on both sides of the conflict. Some of them are new kinds of creatures, but others are simply ones that we meet individually from among groups that we have already seen.

Two of the creatures who are freed from being statues in the Witch's castle stand out from the others. One is the lion who, when Edmund first saw him, seemed to be standing guard at the gate. When he is freed, he can hardly contain his joy or his thankfulness to Aslan. Then, as Aslan calls for him to run in the front with him, his joy is complete.

Giant Rumblebuffin is another interesting character. At first, Susan isn't so sure that it's a good idea to free him since he would be hard to deal with if he turned against them. But Aslan knows best, and Rumblebuffin turns out to be a great guy with the biggest, brightest smile you can imagine. In fact, he turns out to be instrumental in helping them all get through the Witch's gate so that they can go to help Peter and the army fight against the Witch and her followers.

> "'That's what I like about Aslan. No side, no stand-off-ishness. *Us lions*. That meant him and me.'"

What If It Were You?

❋ Have you ever cried so much that you felt like you couldn't cry anymore? What caused it? What did you feel like afterwards?

❋ What do you think Susan and Lucy thought and felt when they first heard Aslan's voice after he came back to life?

❋ How could playing with Aslan be like playing with both a thunderstorm and a kitten? Can you think of any time when you felt two different things like that?

❋ Have you ever ridden a horse? How would you like to ride a lion? What do you think it would be like?

❋ Why was Susan afraid to have Aslan bring the giant to life? Have you ever been afraid of something that turned out to be good for you?

❋ Giant Rumblebuffin was confused when he was first saved from being a statue. What do you think he felt when he finally understood what happened? Can you think of a time when something changed that made life a lot better for you? What did you feel like?

�֍ How do you think Lucy and Susan felt when they saw Edmund and Peter fighting against the Witch?

✷ How do you think that Peter and Edmund felt when they realized that Aslan and the others had come to help them?

✷ When Aslan came back to life, he was able to bring the statues back to life. The Bible says that Jesus brings new life to us. (See Ephesians 4:17-24.) How is that life different from the old life?

✷ FOR OLDER FAMILY MEMBERS: An important part of this portion of the story is the battle between Aslan's army and the Witch's army. How is the Christian life like a battle? Who or what are we fighting? What is necessary for victory? (Read Ephesians 6:10-20 and 1 Timothy 6:11-16 to help your thinking.)

> **Seeing Narnia—**
>
> Notice the changes that take place in the whole atmosphere of the Witch's castle as "the light and the sweet spring air" take over the "dark and evil places."

Eight

THERE AND BACK AGAIN

Chapter 17

The Adventure Concludes

The arrival of Aslan and his followers brings the battle to a quick end. Most of the enemies are killed, and the others run away. Peter tells his friends how it was really Edmund that made victory possible because he broke the Witch's wand. But in fighting against the Witch and her helpers, Edmund has been critically injured.

Aslan reminds Lucy that she has the medicine that can heal Edmund, and she quickly gives him some. She wants to wait to see if he gets better, but there are other wounded members of the army that need her medicine. She goes to the ones who have been injured while Aslan restores those who have been turned to stone.

After spending the night, Aslan, the children, and the others begin the trip eastward along the river toward the castle at Cair Paravel. The castle is different from anything else they have seen in Narnia, full of light and warmth and next to the sea. In the Great Hall, Aslan crowns Peter, Susan, Edmund, and Lucy as kings and queens while everyone cheers.

The description of Cair Paravel and the area around it shows a big difference from the rest of what we see in Narnia. Instead of trees and riverbeds, we have sandy beaches and sea gulls.

The children begin their reigns by giving honors to all of their friends who helped them defeat the Witch and reach this point. Then there is a great feast and a wonderful party to celebrate. But during the party, Aslan slips away quietly, just as Mr. Beaver had warned the children he would do.

Over the next several years, Peter, Susan, Edmund, and Lucy rule over Narnia. They get rid of all of the evil characters there and help the country become all that it is meant to be. In the process, they become adults and don't think any more about their lives back in the other world. In fact, they even begin to talk differently.

Then one day, their old friend Mr. Tumnus brings them word that the White Stag has again been spotted in Narnia. The White Stag is a wonderful creature that will grant wishes to anyone who catches it. Immediately, they all decide to chase after him and try to catch him.

In following the White Stag, they are led into a thicket and come upon a strange metal post with a lantern on top. They start to wonder about it and begin to have the feeling that they have seen it before. They also have the feeling that if they go beyond it, some big change will happen in their lives.

They're right, of course. Soon, they realize that the thing they've seen is the lamppost. Then they realize that they're walking among coats rather than trees. And finally, they come out of the wardrobe and into the spare room of the Professor's house. No time at all has passed since they left.

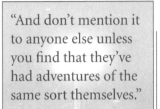

"And don't mention it to anyone else unless you find that they've had adventures of the same sort themselves."

Since they want to explain why four coats are missing from the wardrobe, they tell the Professor what has happened to them. To their surprise, he doesn't doubt it at all, but he tells them he doesn't believe that they can return to Narnia through the wardrobe again.

Still, he feels certain they will return another way.

Did You Know?

Of course, many things in Narnia have seemed miraculous, but in this section, we see a higher concentration of such things. Lucy's medicine heals people no matter how badly they're wounded. Then, there's the fact that Aslan is able to provide food for all of his army seemingly out of nowhere.

In fact, he provides not just any food but a high tea. Most of us are familiar with the idea of a tea party, but for the British, tea includes food. And a high tea is a full meal, similar to what we would think of as supper. Aslan provides for all of their needs. Does that remind you of another story? (Read Matthew 14:13-21.)

As Lewis describes the positive changes that Peter, Susan, Edmund, and Lucy make in Narnia, his humor shows through once again. After mentioning that they remove all of the Witch's followers and keep the good trees from being cut down, Lewis points out that they "liberated" young creatures from being forced to go to school. (Lewis had some negative experiences in boarding school that seem to come out in comments like these.) They also got rid of "busybodies and interferers." Those accomplishments are sure to be ones that bring happiness!

> "Once a king or queen in Narnia, always a king or queen."

The Professor's reaction to what the children tell him (in this section and earlier in the book) surprises them. He doesn't doubt what they say. In fact, he encourages them to believe. Lewis gives us a little bit of a hint about why this might be true. As the Professor talks to the children about the possibility of returning to Narnia in the future, he says, "Once a King in Narnia, always a King in Narnia."

That statement is very similar to what Aslan says when the four children are crowned. But the Professor only mentions one king. Has he heard that statement before used about himself?

Has he been to Narnia before? Is that why he says what he does about how to recognize those who have been there?

In the Family

Big changes come about for Peter, Susan, Edmund, and Lucy in this section. First, we see how Peter and Edmund have changed from their involvement in the battle. Peter appears to be more serious and older when Lucy sees him. But Edmund has changed even more. He has been restored to the way he was not just before he was working with the Witch but even before he went to the school that seemed to change him.

After Lucy gives the medicine to Edmund, she wants to wait to see if he gets better. That seems natural, but Aslan points out to her that she has other responsibilities. Other people are dying, and she can do something about it. She has to make the right use of the gift that she's been given.

Susan and Lucy discuss whether Edmund should be told what Aslan did for him, what the bargain was with the Witch. Susan 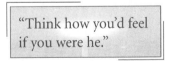 doesn't think so because he would feel too bad if he knew what was done for him. The ironic thing is that the same thing was done for all of us by Christ, so in effect, we all are Edmund.

> "Think how you'd feel if you were he."

When the four grow to be adults and are established as kings and queens, they are given names that show the characteristics that they're known by: King Peter the Magnificent, Queen Susan the Gentle, King Edmund the Just, and Queen Lucy the Valiant.

The People We Meet

Throughout the adventure, we have heard about the castle at Cair Paravel, and we have been reminded that we were getting closer and closer. We even got a glimpse of it from far away. But when we actually see it, it lives up to all the anticipation. It's a wonderful palace that is filled with beautiful things.

It has a gate that opens right onto the sea, and through that gate, we're introduced to some new creatures: mermaids and mermen. Of course, they can't come into the woods, so they haven't been a part of the battle, but they share in the celebration and sing their own song for the new kings and queens.

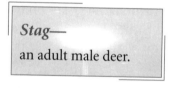

Stag—

an adult male deer.

The final chapter of the story is named for a final character. The White Stag plays an important part in the adventure. First of all, he represents the idea of meeting a challenge and not being afraid. Secondly, he leads the children back to their home world. Has he been sent by Aslan for just that purpose?

What If It Were You?

❋ If you had Lucy's medicine, what would you do with it?

❋ Would you have wanted to wait, as Lucy did, to see how Edmund was before you went to help others?

❋ Susan and Lucy were worried about how Edmund would feel about what Aslan had done for him. How do you feel about what Jesus has done for you?

❋ What do you remember about the description of Cair Paravel? Can you imagine other things about what it looked like?

❋ How do you think the children felt when they were crowned as kings and queens? Do you think they were scared at all?

❋ Why do you think that Aslan left the way he did, without saying anything to anyone? How do you think the children felt when they realized he was gone?

> "He's wild, you know. Not like a tame lion."

❋ We are told about the names that are given to Peter, Susan, Edmund, and Lucy after they have been kings and queens a long time. What names do you think might be given to each member of our family to describe us?

❋ What do you think the children felt when they realized they were back in the Professor's house? What do you think was the first thing they did?

❋ The book ends by saying that it was the "end of the adventures of the wardrobe" but possibly "only the beginning of the adventures of Narnia." What do you think might happen next?

❋ FOR OLDER FAMILY MEMBERS: The Professor gives the children advice on how to deal with their experience in terms of talking about it with other people. How does what he tells them relate to how we should talk about our relationship with Christ to other people? What similarities and differences do you see? (See Ephesians 6:19, 20 and 1 Peter 3:14-17 to help you think about our responsibility.)

Nine

ONE FOR ALL AND
ALL IN ONE

The Adventure ҂ a Summary

Two brothers (Peter and Edmund) and their sisters (Susan and Lucy) have been sent to the country to stay with a professor. In exploring their new surroundings, they find a spare room that has nothing in it but a wardrobe.

Lucy is the first to discover that the wardrobe contains an entrance to a world called Narnia. While there, she meets a faun named Mr. Tumnus who tells her a little bit about life there before he admits to her that he has been assigned by the White Witch to capture any human who comes to Narnia. The Witch is the evil ruler of Narnia, who has made it so that it is always winter and never Christmas. However, Mr. Tumnus can't go through with the plan and lets Lucy go.

The others don't believe Lucy's story because the wardrobe appears to be ordinary when they push back the coats and look at the back.

Later, Lucy enters Narnia again, and this time, Edmund follows her. He meets the White Witch, and she wins him to her side by giving him some enchanted Turkish Delight and promising to make him a prince if he brings his brother and sisters to her.

When Lucy and Edmund return, Edmund won't admit that he's been to Narnia. In fact, he keeps getting meaner and meaner. Peter and Susan talk to the Professor to get his advice about what should be done for Lucy and are surprised to hear him say that he thinks they should believe her.

Finally, the children all enter Narnia together, and Lucy leads the others to Mr. Tumnus's house, which has been destroyed. A note tells them that the faun has been captured because he is a traitor to the Queen. The children decide to do what they can to try to save Mr. Tumnus.

After following a robin into the woods, the children are met by Mr. Beaver, who leads them to his home. He and his wife take care of them and tell them all about Narnia and about Aslan, the Lion King of Narnia who is said to be returning after many years away. Mr. Beaver has been assigned to take the children to meet Aslan.

Edmund, after hearing of the plans, sneaks away to the Witch's house, hoping for some more Turkish Delight and to get revenge for the wrong that he believes the others have done to him. When he gets to her castle, though, he's not sure that he's made a good choice because it's a horrible place, and the Witch is mean to him.

The Beavers take Peter, Susan, and Lucy toward the Stone Table, where they are to meet Aslan, while the Witch takes Edmund with her in hopes of heading off the others and killing them. However, since the Witch is traveling by sleigh, her progress is slowed by the thaw that is taking place since Aslan has returned.

The children are met on the way by Father Christmas, further evidence that the Witch is losing control of Narnia. He gives gifts to Peter, Susan, and Lucy that they are to use for specific purposes. Edmund also sees evidence of Father Christmas when he and the Witch come upon a group celebrating with the food that Father Christmas has brought them.

When the Witch turns the whole group into stone, a positive change begins to take place in Edmund.

Aslan is waiting at the Stone Table when the Beavers and the three children arrive. All that they've been told isn't enough to prepare them for how wonderful and powerful Aslan is. He greets them and has them begin to prepare themselves for what is to come. In the midst of preparations, Peter is called upon to kill Fenris Ulf, a wolf who serves as the Witch's captain of the guard and who has trapped Susan in a tree.

Meanwhile, the Witch has decided to kill Edmund to be sure that there are not four humans to sit on the four thrones at the castle of Cair Paravel (fulfilling a prophecy that would mean the end of her life). But at the last minute, a group of Aslan's followers arrives to save Edmund.

The four children are happy to be reunited, but that happiness doesn't last long because the next day the Witch comes to their camp. She claims that she has the right to kill Edmund because the Deep Magic that governs Narnia gives her the right to kill someone every time a betrayal happens (as Edmund had betrayed his brother and sisters).

Aslan offers to take Edmund's place, and the Witch is overjoyed. Susan and Lucy watch from a hiding place as the Witch and her evil followers torture and kill the great Lion. The Witch thinks she has triumphed because not only has she killed Aslan, but she has also removed his protection from the others, so she can kill them, too.

However, the next morning, Aslan comes back to life because of a deeper magic that comes from a time before the Witch. He has Susan and Lucy get on his back, and they hurry to free those that the Witch has turned into stone at her castle. Then they all join Peter, Edmund, and the others who are battling against the Witch. When they arrive, things aren't going so well, but Aslan takes care of the Witch, and that turns the battle around, so the good side wins.

After the victory, Aslan and his followers all travel to the castle of Cair Paravel, which is on the sea. There, Aslan crowns Peter, Susan, Edmund, and Lucy as kings and queens. The four rule for many years in Narnia, getting rid of evil and helping the country to become happy and free.

Then, when the four have become adults, they are told that the White Stag, a magical creature that can grant wishes, has been spotted in Narnia. They form a group to chase after the Stag, who eventually leads them back to their own world. When they arrive there, they find that no time has passed since they left.

Did You Know?

Different aspects of C. S. Lewis's life help us to understand more about the book. The very situation described at the beginning, with children being sent to stay in the country, happened to him. During World War II, the city of London was bombed almost nightly, so many families sent their children to stay in safer places. Lewis had some of those children stay in his home.

The fact that Lewis was British adds focus to the way he uses kings and queens in the story. It makes the whole possibility more realistic. Also, the talk about having tea and eating high tea, which is a late afternoon or evening meal, point to the British culture as well. Some British homes are also used for tours, as the Professor's is.

Finally, the character of the Professor may have been based on Lewis himself. He was, indeed, a college professor with a home in the country. So when Lewis talks about the Professor being funny looking and a bit odd, he may be making a joke about himself.

As we mentioned in the introduction, Lewis wasn't trying to make a direct connection between the story of our salvation in Christ and what happens in Narnia, but he was supposing what God would do to save a world like Narnia if such a place existed. That makes it interesting to see the elements that he thinks would stay the same even if the world changed.

Prophecies predict Aslan's coming just as prophecies predicted the coming of Christ. Aslan is a willing sacrifice just as Jesus was. The forces of evil seem to be winning, but that all changes when Aslan comes back from the dead. Jesus' victory over death offers salvation to all of us. And Peter, Susan, Edmund, and Lucy sit on the four thrones of Cair Paravel just as the Bible says that we will reign with Christ (2 Timothy 2:12).

In the Family

Peter is the oldest child in the family and seems to be the natural leader. However, at times, he takes his leadership a little for granted and walks over the others a bit. Later, he recognizes that fault and admits that it contributed to Edmund's problems. Peter takes leadership in Aslan's army and proves himself to be brave and strong. Later, he is called King Peter the Magnificent by the people of Narnia.

Susan seems a bit timid at times, but she is also very practical. When Mr. Beaver is calling them into the woods, she is the one who says that they'll have to take the chance on him because they don't have any other options. With Lucy, she cares for Aslan's dead body and then shares the joy when he comes back to life. Maybe it's that kind of care that led to her being called Queen Susan the Gentle.

Edmund has a bad case of envy. He sees that Peter is the leader of the family, and Edmund doesn't like it. When the Witch offers him the opportunity to be a prince, he sees it immediately as a way to be more important than Peter. Edmund seems to have what is often referred to as middle-child syndrome, and he is trying to find a place of importance that he doesn't think he has.

Of course, he goes about it all wrong and betrays his family. The irony with how we view Edmund is that he's the negative one in the family, but he's the one that we should connect to. We're the reason Jesus had to die just as Aslan had to die for Edmund. So we're very glad when Edmund repents and fights on the right side. He's the one who breaks the Witch's wand and makes winning the battle possible. In the end, he seems to deserve the title of King Edmund the Just.

Lucy, who shares a name with C. S. Lewis's goddaughter to whom the book is dedicated, is curious and adventurous and very trusting. She makes the first connection to Narnia and forms the friendship with Mr. Tumnus that leads to the children's seeking to free him after he has been captured by the Witch. She faces problems when even those she loves don't believe her, but she sticks by the truth, and eventually, she is proved right. She has a very close relationship with Aslan and never seems to lose her adventurous nature. That's why the people of Narnia call her Queen Lucy the Valiant.

The way the children interact teaches us many lessons. We see the importance of being truthful no matter what. Through Edmund, we learn how easy it is to be led in the wrong direction when we are selfish. We learn about forgiveness in what happens after Edmund is sorry. And we see commitment and determination in many aspects of what they do.

The People We Meet

THE LION

By the title of the book and by the plot of the story, we know how important Aslan is to Narnia. We begin hearing about him long before we meet him. His name appears in prophecies, and people in Narnia just expect that everyone knows who he is. And even if people don't know him (like Peter, Susan, Edmund, and Lucy), when they hear his name, they react to it.

Several of Aslan's character qualities are emphasized for us. The Beavers are quite upset to even consider the idea that he is human, and they respond in a similar way to the question of whether he's tame. In fact, several times we're told that he's not tame; he can't be controlled or limited by others. However, he is good.

Throughout the story, a careful point is made to balance Aslan's power and his goodness. He should never be taken for granted, but those who are on his side have nothing to fear from him. Because of his power, when the children first meet him, no one wants to speak first. But as soon as Aslan speaks, they all feel completely at ease around him.

Central to the message of the story is the fact that Aslan makes himself a willing sacrifice in Edmund's place. Through that action, he not only saves Edmund but also ends the Witch's power. He also offers Edmund complete forgiveness in the situation and expects the others to do the same.

In spite of his power (shown in his roar) and his miracles (such as bringing the statues back to life), Aslan is very unassuming and jumps right in to fight among all the rest. And in the midst of the celebration, he quietly goes on his way to leave Peter, Susan, Edmund, and Lucy to finish the job.

The Witch

As with Aslan, we hear about the Witch before we meet her.

Mr. Tumnus warns Lucy of the evil force the witch is and how she treats the people of Narnia. When Edmund arrives, we get a contrasting picture as he meets a woman who calls herself Queen and gives gifts to Edmund.

However, it doesn't take long for us to be sure that they're the same person as we see that the so-called Queen doesn't really deserve to rule the country and is certainly not nice. Mr.

Beaver explains that she is only pretending to be human but is really one of the Jinn, descended from Adam's first wife. (For more on these legends, see chapter five of this book.)

While the Witch isn't all that she pretends to be, she does have some power. She has a wand that makes her able to turn others into stone. She also has the ability to make things seem like things that they aren't. And she can use tricks like the enchanted Turkish Delight to make people do what she wants them to do. But it doesn't take long for people who think she's going to help them to learn the truth. She's really only interested in how she can use them.

AND THE OTHERS

The followers of Aslan and the Witch contain all kinds of creatures. In fact, many of the creatures are taken from many different sources.

There are animals that we're familiar with such as beavers, wolves, eagles, and (of course) lions. From the realm of mythology come Dryads (tree nymphs), Naiads (water nymphs), fauns (half man/half goat), and centaurs (half man/half horse). Dwarfs, ogres, giants, mermaids, and other creatures come from legends and fairy tales. Even the trees are participants in the story. All categories are represented on both sides of the division of good and evil.

Some characters stand out from the group. On the good side, the Beavers make a strong impression in the way that they care for the children and lead them to Aslan. They also teach the children what they need to know about Aslan and about his power to save. Giant Rumblebuffin and another lion are among those that Aslan frees from being statues, and they stand out as eager and thankful followers.

The first follower of the Witch we meet is the dwarf who drives her sleigh. The Witch certainly seems to trust him, but when he tries to offer her advice, she makes very clear that he is just a slave and not an advisor. Another servant of the Witch is Fenris Ulf, the wolf who is the captain of her guard. He also is a trusted follower, but she doesn't hesitate to give him assignments that ultimately lead to his death.

A few characters are not connected with just one side of the battle. Mr. Tumnus is different because he begins on one side (the Witch's) but changes to the other due to the influence that Lucy has in his life. Father Christmas, better known to us as Santa Claus, isn't a part of the battle, but he is clearly good. His coming represents the beginning of the end of the Witch and the announcing of the coming of Aslan. He also gives very important gifts to Peter, Susan, Edmund, and Lucy.

What If It Were You?

❋ How are the relationships among Peter, Susan, Edmund, and Lucy like the ones in our family? How are they different?

❋ What do you think it was like for Lucy when she first discovered that she was in a different world inside the wardrobe? How would you have felt? Would you have gone on or gone back?

❋ How did the Witch fool Edmund into thinking she was a Queen? What lessons can we learn about not trusting everyone who tells us something? How can we be sure that what we're hearing is the truth?

❋ Why did Edmund decide to lie about having been in Narnia? Have you ever been tempted to lie just to play a joke on someone or to get back at someone? How did it turn out?

❋ Would you have trusted the Beavers the way that the children did? How did Mr. Beaver let them know that they could trust him?

❋ What things did the children learn about Aslan before they met him? Would you have wanted to meet Aslan? Do you think you would have been a little afraid the way the children were at first?

❋ What did Edmund think about when he was going to meet the Witch? Did he like what he saw when he got to her castle? Why do you think he went in anyway?

❋ Have you ever had anyone hurt you the way that Edmund hurt his brother and sisters? How did you feel about that person when it happened? Did you forgive the person later?

❋ What gifts did Father Christmas give to Peter, Susan, Edmund, and Lucy? Why were they given those gifts? Do you think that you have been given things that you can use in important ways?

❀ How does what Aslan did for Edmund remind you of what Jesus did for us? What about the way both of them came back to life and what happened after?

❀ What do you think are the most important lessons we can learn from this book?

❀ Which one of the characters do you think that you're most like? Why?

❀ For older family members: If you were going to create a world in which to tell a story of evil, betrayal, goodness, and redemption, what would you put into that world? What kinds of places and characters would be part of that world?

❀ How is the situation of Edmund and the Witch (with her enchanted Turkish Delight) similar to what we experience with temptation and sin? What develops in the process of sin? What can happen to change our perspective? Use Scriptures such as John 8:34, 35 and James 1:14-16 to help you consider the connection.

❀ The last segment of the story focuses on the battle between Aslan's army and the Witch's army. How is the Christian life like a battle? Who or what are we fighting? What is necessary for victory? (Read Ephesians 6:10-20 and 1 Timothy 6:11-16 to help your thinking.)

Read the book . . .

See the movie . . .

Dig deep

And share with your children the awesome spiritual truths of hope, love, grace, and redemption.

Finally! Here's real-life help for busy parents who want to teach their kids about important things such as how to save money, why respecting others is essential, why some music is dangerous to our minds, what connection there is between our attitudes and behaviors, and the toughest of all—where do babies come from? **The I Want to Teach My Child About...** series is here to help with clear, concise guidance, real-life hints and helps, quick-tips and checklists, and loads more. Check out all these exciting books for busy parents—because you're never too busy to teach your child!

I Want to Teach My Child About MONEY
ISBN 0784717621

I Want to Teach My Child About MANNERS
ISBN 0784717702

I Want to Teach My Child About SEX
ISBN 0784717613

I Want to Teach My Child About VALUES
ISBN 078471763X

I Want to Teach My Child About MEDIA
ISBN 0784717699

I Want to Teach My Child About FITNESS
ISBN 0784717648